THE INSPIRED HOME

THE
INSPIRED
HOME
Nests of
Creatives

Kim Ficaro & Todd Nickey
Photography by Ditte Isager

with Texts by Mayer Rus &
Sarah Sophie Flicker

RIZZOLI
NEW YORK

New York · Paris · London · Milan

TABLE OF CONTENTS

FINDING HOME
By Kim Ficaro &
Todd Nickey

Our concept for this book came from a place of genuine curiosity and a passion to explore the stories of people we admire. We set out with a singular mission: to showcase a group of people that we knew, or knew of, whose inspiring personal style translated to their homes. Just as the wind and sand can affect the surface of a mountain, each home has the indelible imprint of their creators' spirit and style.

This was a lengthy process, one with many unexpected detours. We wanted to be fully immersed in their worlds and found that we had very sensitive reactions to each space and subject. It was emotional and visceral, a journey in the truest sense of the word. Our approach was not to prescribe or champion a particular aesthetic, it was purely about telling a beautiful story about how these people live, and the thoughtful choices they make.

Our daily work lives are primarily about lending our taste and style to a particular venue: a catalogue, a house, a restaurant, a shop... it's a very outward-facing, public endeavor. Regardless of a project's success or appeal, our job is to infuse it with our creative ideas. This book gave us the opportunity to look through a different lens. It let us appreciate the beauty and composition of what was in front of us, without our input. In this way, we were allowed to let the material breathe on its own; to go into someone's home and find the great shots, just as it is, no styling.

With that in mind, our hope is to portray as honestly as possible the intentions our subjects had when building their homes—to convey that specificity, that point of view—and to examine the idea of home as an expression of character.

Some of these expressions are nuanced, and others are quite obvious. Christiane Perrechon's subtle use of the colors of her ceramic glazes throughout her home and studio in Tuscany are a natural communion of her art and life.

Rogan Gregory's house is filled with simple and soothing colors and creations from his workshop, allowing him to constantly be around the physical elements that he transformed into functional objects.

We wanted the reader to discover what we did—that anything is possible and there is no set standard. What is a home, anyway? Is it a sanctuary from a frenetic artistic life, such as Curtis Kulig's downtown loft; a warm, whimsical harbor for family and social gatherings, such as Mads and Cecilie Nørgaard's magical houseboat in Copenhagen; or is it a calming beach retreat, such as Athena and Victor Calderone's Amagansett abode? No matter what the function of the home, we were constantly amazed at how it was infused with the inhabitant's individual personality and style, this idea that one is an extension of another.

Finally, using the nest as metaphor gave us an opportunity to categorize our subjects in a more abstract way. We wanted to create a figurative gallery for their works to be displayed without the confines of literal definitions of "house" or "apartment." This way, we sought to reveal the true nature of what makes a home a home, a place of serenity, safety, community, and love; and to convey the intangible beauty of the places we all come home to.

We have been blessed with an amazing group of collaborators and subjects and are extremely grateful for their participation. We hope to have captured the true essence of each through photographer Ditte Isager's palpable light, and to have revealed how every layer, every choice, comes from a place of true intuition, imagination, insight, and listening to their own voice.

This is our flock... and these are their nests.

TASTE THIS
By Mayer Rus

Nature vs. nurture? Nurture vs. nature? In matters of style, there's no magical formula or lofty theory that explains why some people are blessed with extraordinary, idiosyncratic personal taste. Philosophers from Plato and Confucius to Kant and Schopenhauer have wrestled with the vicissitudes and vagaries of aesthetics for millennia. Sociologists have likewise tried to map the strange terrain of beauty and taste by studying those elusive concepts through the lens of social class, economics, and matrices of consumption. But the simple truth remains that that there are certain individuals who seem to be born with innate aesthetic discernment—a kind of daring vision that comes to life most dramatically in the design of their homes.

Facile hypotheses regarding the origins of taste have never been in short supply. One of the more dubious of these—the nature argument—posits that aesthetic sensibilities are tied to genetics. But the idea that imagination and inspiration are somehow encoded in one's DNA contradicts the ample evidence provided by countless scions of acknowledged geniuses and celebrated artists who have labored without success in the same fields as their illustrious forebears.

Then there's the nurture argument, which delves into childhood environs and cultural exposure to track the roots of taste. It would be ludicrous to suggest that personal history has no effect on the formation of aesthetic sensibility, but it's equally absurd to believe that environment or education alone can explain why some people possess a weird and wonderful eye for beauty, totally original, while others wallow in slavish devotion to trends and fashion. How can one explain the innumerable tastemakers and aesthetes who were raised on the wrong side of the tracks (to borrow a quaint but evocative expression), or those titans of taste whose formative years were spent in the suffocating surrounds of stale, bourgeois nothingness?

For this book, authors Kim Ficaro and Todd Nickey have wisely avoided any pseudo-authoritative taxonomies of taste and instead concocted a fanciful avian framework (night owls, sandpipers, mourning doves, etc.) to present the well-feathered nests of their subjects. In terms of style, it's a far-flung group, but the majority are creative directors, stylists, artists, and designers—folks who have parlayed their distinctive sensibilities into viable careers. Beyond their adventurous aesthetic sensibilities, the tie that binds them is their capacity for making homes of remarkable grace, beauty, and power.

This book isn't the typical entry in the shelter-porn category, that vast confiserie of delectable design compendia that tantalize readers through fantasy projection, aspiration, desire, and voyeurism. Although the bulk of homes belong to so-called "creative types," the owners are, for the most part, not professional interior designers. They don't conjure signature looks or visions of domestic bliss for paying clients, and the homes they've built don't lend themselves easily to reproduction or classification.

Take, for example, the ethereal Manhattan redoubt of artist and shopkeeper John Derian. There are, to be sure, plenty of decorating lessons to be gleaned from this dreamy domicile—nobody works a smudged wall and a decrepit radiator quite like Derian—but that's not really the point. Ditte Isager's seductive photographs are not meant to be exhaustive chronicles of home design that attempt to depict every room, chair, artwork, and wall covering. Instead, her impressionistic images, more poetic than documentary in nature, are an invitation to ponder the singular spirit of one particular person and place. The bird metaphors are therefore decidedly apt—Isager's pictures offer insight into elusive flights of fancy and arabesques of imagination not easily captured in traditional interiors photography.

And while the name John Derian might strike a chord for aficionados of design, the other homeowners included in this volume are generally not boldface names (Moby notwithstanding), despite the considerable influence many exert on popular culture as behind-the-scenes brand wizards and style gurus. Their inclusion here says as much about the tastes and sensibilities of the authors as it does about the subjects themselves. Ficaro and Nickey clearly prize eccentric personal vision above hackneyed notions of grandeur or glamour—a point of view that is as rare as it is inspiring.

If there's one big takeaway from this book, it's the challenge it issues to craft our homes as true reflections of who we are, places that embrace the kaleidoscopic wonders of art, design, and nature as part of an ongoing exercise in decorative autobiography. That's the very best kind of taste, the one that matters most.

GO HOME AGAIN
By Sarah Sophie Flicker

It is said that you can never go home again, and maybe you can't. Maybe childhood memories can never live up to their present-day realities, but I am intent on trying.

For me, a home is many things. It's a place to create, a place to be cozy and feel safe, a place for gatherings... but mostly it is a place for memories. A main job as a parent is to be a memory-making machine. Selfishly, I want my kids to have such wonderful, warm, love-filled memories that they do, in fact, want to go home again—and again, and again.

Our home is a collaboration. I say this in the sense that my husband and I agreed early on not to bring anything into our home that we didn't both love. This generally applies to most things in our relationship. It's become a mantra that we both adhere to; in people, in objects, in life. I view life itself as a collaboration— the idea that we are lonely pioneers thrashing our way through the wild fields of being never appealed to me.

When I was younger, I assumed this was a sign of weakness on my part or a lack of belief in my singular ideals. I've always looked to other people for work, be it through my theater work with The Citizens Band or my collaborative film and political projects, I always look for a sense of community. Perhaps this is a result of my upbringing. I was born in Copenhagen and spent the bulk of my early years visiting my mother's best friend who lived in Christiania, a military base taken over by radicals in the early 1970s to create a communal "free city" with a leadership and aesthetic outside the Danish status quo. Whatever the root cause, I've spent my life looking for an extended family, a group larger than my immediate blood relations.

In meeting and marrying my husband Jesse—also a highly social human who loves to be surrounded by friends, family, music, laughter, and food—we found a match. Being with Jesse and creating our own "village," I've found a way of living that makes me happy. It sounds obvious but research shows time and again that the root of happiness is in community. The root of happiness is loving and being loved, and sharing your life with people who also share common values.

The concept of common values is very important to our home life. Many people actually refer to our apartment as "The Village" because it is host to dinner parties, impromptu hang-outs, and political discussions—it is also a rehearsal hall, neighborhood cafe, and haven. In fact, during the New York City blackout of 2003, a group of about twenty-five friends came to our apartment (we were out of town) and proceeded to eat, drink, and be merry, even without their usual hosts, because that is the kind of welcoming place it is.

Our home is filled with items that mean something. I love the idea of "meaning" behind objects, that the things we have are a representation of what we believe and what matters to us. Everything we have should be touched, admired, played with, well loved, well worn, irreplaceable yet completely nonprecious. For us it's never been a plan or a theme or a designer or an interior decorator, it's a collection of things that speak to us, and because they speak our aesthetic language, the objects communicate well together. I never really know what I'm looking for, I just know it when I see it. Something that is from my tribe of interests and likes. I see it and I think, "Ah, there's one!"

I've always believed that home is anywhere the people I love reside. What makes this apartment magical isn't anything quantifiable, visual, or tangible, it is the life that has been lived here. And I love this space for that life and will forever be grateful to these walls for housing such cherished moments. But I also believe that our love and lives travel with us.

We are moving out of our much-loved apartment, the place where my happiest moments have occurred and my most monumental life changes have transpired. It is the place where I fell in love, where I created my proudest work. Where I became a woman. Where I carried my three children. Where I brought them home and felt more love than I ever thought possible. This is both a sad moment and a thrilling one.

Much like generations before us have aspired to do, we are now in the midst of creating our dream home. We've found a broken-down spot that we are now intent on resurrecting to its former glory. A place where our children can play outside, where they can walk to visit friends and family. A place that houses all our hopes for the future—as not just a shelter but as an extension of our family itself. Most importantly, we are building a place where memories will be made ad infinitum, a permanent memory-making machine.

We are creating rooms and spaces now built on all we know of what a thriving "village" requires. I think, because of our informal rule that we both must love what enters our home, we've learned to let go of things that speak only to our personal interests but somehow are a true representation of the other person. Certainly my husband makes room for my obsessions with cabaret, circus, anything old-timey and silly. And I make room for his love of all things epicurean and kitchen-oriented. But when I look around, it all works. That's the magic of well-loved items. We have no agenda other than a cozy one.

True, I want our home to be the safest place, the warmest place, the most magical place and, in my heart of hearts, the place that my children will always want to come home to. This can exist anywhere that we are, because we create it, not from premeditation but from intuition and love.

As a kid, my happiest memories are of lying in bed and listening to my parents and their friends laughing through the night, glasses and dinnerware clinking, the smell of food, wine, and, at the time, cigarettes, the sounds of jazz playing and intense conversation. I remember trying to concoct ways to go out, tussle-headed and pajama-clad, for just a few more minutes in their celebration of nothing else but friendship.

Our kids do the same thing now. I love to watch them pass from lap to lap of friends, knowing that those relationships will nourish the parts of them that their parents can't. No one person can be everything. This truth is another reason why I love collaboration. My husband has the same memories, and without discussing them, we set out to create the same ideals for our kids: To live in a home surrounded by interesting, strange, creative people. An extended family of folks who they can turn to later in life when they, inevitably, feel they can't turn to us.

Our feeling is, if we are fortunate enough to have this wonderful space, our duty is to share it with the people we love. Nothing makes me happier than a candlelit table surrounded by the people I find most inspiring. James Baldwin said, "Perhaps home is not a place but simply an irrevocable condition." I love that. The condition being a sense of belonging and safety. From our village to yours, happy homemaking!

Sarah Sophie Flicker lives
in New York City—she is
a mother, wife, trapeze artist,
and founding member/creative
director of The Citizens Band.
She is the editor at large to
Lula magazine, a contributor
to *Rookie* magazine and
HelloGiggles, and she works
as a film/PSA directing team
with Maximilla Lukacs.

Clockwise from top left: Sarah
Sophie Flicker is photographed
in her West Village studio
surrounded by her collection
of vintage tutus, ballet shoes,
and memorabilia; a wall of
cards and mementoes; vintage
ballet slippers.

Equal parts solemn and sprightly, the mourning dove is known for its lovely lamentlike warble. Slender-tailed with gray and brown plumage, its flight pattern is arrow-straight. When a mourning dove alights, all sense of timidity vanishes; it is transformed from a creature of quiet contemplation to one of bright, bold action.

The three homes we discover here and their inhabitants share this duality— at once vessels of thoughtful restraint and wild, joyous activity.

Chapter 1

MOURNING DOVES

RICHARD FERRETTI &
JAMES GAGER

"Global creative director" isn't merely a job—it is a way of life, a driving impulse to curate, refine, and beautify. Richard Ferretti, global creative director for Esteé Lauder, and James Gager, global creative director at MAC cosmetics, have combined their considerable artistic acumen to create a home away from home in New Hope, Pennsylvania.

They split their time between New York City and New Hope, where they reside in an eighteenth-century stone house. As one would expect of two creative perfectionists, the décor is meticulous.

"The colors of our house in Pennsylvania are based on a very simple palette of white and gray," Gager explains. "The white has a bit of chalkiness to it with undertones of pale, pale, gray and a darker charcoal gray. We like the idea of simplicity, keeping everything as neutral as possible."

Against this clean-slate backdrop, Ferretti and Gager have developed a style that's completely their own. Wandering through the living room, kitchen, sitting room, three bedrooms, and a spacious third-floor living space (it was formerly a painter's studio), one sees an amalgamation of impeccably restored furniture, pottery, art, and graceful oddities. There's a common thread in both tone and texture that creates a calming, harmonious whole.

This makes sense—at the helm of their respective beauty brands, Ferretti and Gager work with eye-popping palettes every day. "An environment that doesn't shout color is a wonderful relief," Gager says.

This is true of the grounds as well, which resemble a smartly landscaped park. The exterior of an adjacent barn is white with a subtly sooty trim. Yet nothing feels fussy or mannered, instead it all evokes a cozy austerity. This less-is-more design aesthetic is also an ideal showcase for the ample natural beauty on the property. The barn is surrounded by trees and flowers that provide their own visual fireworks, from soft summer blooms to blazing autumn leaves. It's the perfect antidote to their hectic Manhattan professional lives.

"There are endless things I love in the house," Ferretti says. "Each room is a favorite in some way. It's all about how things go together and how you feel when you are in the space."

Gager echoes this sentiment: "I know when people visit for the first time, they feel a very 'Zen' quality to our space. Maybe that reflects Richard and me as a couple, I'm not really sure. It certainly makes us happy and keeps us at peace."

The guest bedroom at Ferretti and Gager's eighteenth-century farm in New Hope, Pennsylvania. Their palette of chalky white and gray creates an environment that emphasizes simplicity and calm. The house is filled with a very specific amalgamation of antiques and modern pieces that encapsulates their aesthetic.

Opposite: The upstairs living room was formerly a painter's studio. Antlers sit atop the nineteenth-century drafting table. *Top left:* The center hall stairwell of the farmhouse is simple and unadorned. The banister and chair rail are painted the same charcoal color. The floors throughout are stripped and waxed, emphasizing the natural beauty of the two-hundred-year-old wood. A gray and white lotus-patterned wallpaper is on walls throughout the stairwell and landings.

Top right: A burnished steel tub is the focal point of the guest bathroom. A shag rug is juxtaposed with the wide plank floors. *Following spread, left:* A metal cutout framed piece (actually a lamp) is placed above a primitive bench. *Following spread, right:* The center table of the kitchen flanked by industrial chairs and a gold-leafed antler stool.

Previous spread: The eighteenth-century basement of the barn/living space. A velvet settee and dining chairs flank a long farm table. *Top left:* The creative masters James Gager (standing) and Richard Ferretti photographed on the top floor of their barn, as light filters through the slatted walls.

Top right: A nineteenth-century portrait is hung above a set of Gustavian chairs in the barn's basement. The wall is constructed of local limestone. *Opposite:* A still life in the root cellar; an old wallpapering table is set as a desk with modern sculptural chair.

CHRISTINE RUDOLPH

Christine Rudolph is a sought-after set designer and interior and prop stylist, but some of her most striking work can be found off the page. Her primary residence, an eighteenth-century house in Copenhagen, Denmark, is a testament to her precise yet playful eye.

Rudolph's fluency with color and texture is almost hypnotic. The dominant palette is dove white, creating a sense of sparseness and simplicity. For a secondary palette, spaces are shot through with inky black and powder blue, giving each room a sense of depth, dimension, and near-Jacobean intrigue.

This grasp of the ethereal and narrative mirrors her editorial work in magazines such as *Elle Decoration*, *Vogue Living Australia*, and *Elle Decor Italy*, as well as advertising campaigns for H&M and Fritz Hanson, and in the award-winning cookbook *Noma: Time and Place in Nordic Cuisine* by René Redzepi.

Not quite rustic, not quite minimalist, there's a definite precision to her choices. Every piece of furniture, wall color, and piece of art appears to be humming with life and utterly inviting.

In some sense her aesthetic is a polite rebuke of hyperstylized, Photoshop-perfect spaces one sees in shelter magazines. Rudolph doesn't overstyle her spaces, her disparate collections of ceramic pots, bowls, and pitchers sit out on random surfaces, books are piled sky-high, sketches and photographs are taped to the walls at odd angles. The phrase "beautiful accident" seems to apply.

In the dining room, a hodgepodge of mid-century modern chairs sit amiably around a wooden dining room table, itself salvaged from a horse's stable. The open floor plan allows for further improvisation: gauzy curtains demarcate a bedroom, an oversize wreath of branches casually graces a wall, and wicker baskets hang off exposed wood beams.

It's like entering a new world, or more accurately, an old one, something from a fairytale, where the lost child always turns up safe before a warm hearth. During the day, the diffuse Denmark sunlight filters through the East-facing windows, while at night, the interior shades of blue and inky black are bathed in layers of soft lighting.

The organization of objects has a purist's sensibility yet it is light and inviting—one wants to just collapse on the pewter-colored sofa, or perch on wooden stools in the kitchen for hours, glass of wine in hand.

Throughout every square foot of the space, Rudolph captures the idea of home as a place for both respite and renewal, where new ideas are born, traditions maintained, and everything has its place.

Stacks of books are part of set-designer Rudolph's work/living space. The leather-covered campaign butterfly chair is as beautiful as it is comfortable. The white floors throughout offer a bright and clean backdrop.

Opposite: The workspace in the former carriage house is simple and makeshift. Sawhorses and a wooden plank create a desk that is covered with inspiring objects; the walls display photos as color studies. Files of feathers, trims, and other necessary objects are neatly stacked. *Right:* Rudolph, photographed in the courtyard against a vine-draped wall, with her bicycle—a must-have for daily life in Copenhagen.

MOBY

Enter the Wolf's Lair. Perched on the edge of Beachwood Canyon in Los Angeles, this Norman micro-castle was built in the 1920s, taking its name from the original owner, real estate magnate L. Milton Wolf. Over the years it has played host to countless Hollywood luminaries, from Bugsy Siegel to Marlon Brando and the Rolling Stones.

Today it is home to Moby—singer, songwriter, producer, DJ, photographer, pioneering vegan, Lower East Side teahouse entrepreneur, and bona fide electronic music legend (just listen to 1999's *Play* again and marvel at how deeply it has permeated pop culture).

He spends time in his self-described "Nordic Gothic" home spreading his prodigious talents by working with young artists; producing, writing, recording, and hopefully nurturing the next generation of Mobys. He is also passionate about design and architecture, and was deeply involved with the restoration and interior concepts of his home.

Inside and out, the spaces communicate a rich sense of old Hollywood élan without a hint of vintage oppressiveness. Credit the modernist quietude of the muted palette and the views down the bucolic ridges of Beachwood Canyon and up the hill to the iconic Hollywood sign.

To achieve a contemporary feel without forsaking the soul of the Wolf's Lair, Moby hired Tim Barber, Ltd, a Los Angeles–based architecture firm, to conduct a full-scale restoration, which entailed adding three bathrooms, replacing the roof, gutting the kitchen, replacing windows, and stripping down extraneous decorative elements to reveal its original beauty.

Moby christened the finished product a "crazy shining castle" in the *New York Times*, but there's nothing off-the-wall about the refined interior. Exposed wood-beamed ceilings, eggshell white walls, and tawny upholstery give the space an almost monastic quality.

He painstakingly chose the furniture—all impeccable Scandinavian and American mid-century modern pieces—which design die-hards would kill for. Yet there's also a sense of not taking himself too seriously: on the kitchen wall there's a signed drawing of Homer Simpson, and throughout the living room one finds scores of antique globes, including a Day-Glow aquamarine astrology globe.

Canyon views beckon outside just about every window and the grounds feature a classic kidney-shaped pool and sprawling foliage, like a deliriously overgrown English garden. Across the lawn is a guesthouse, originally designed by Frank Lloyd Wright protégé John Lautner in 1961. Moby converted the guesthouse garage to a state-of-the-art recording studio where artists can lay down tracks in privacy. Unconventional, unpretentious, and unexpected, it's the ideal space for this multitalented artist to work, entertain, relax, and reflect—a castle fit for a cerebral king.

A full-length window in the dining room of Moby's 1920s "micro-castle" affords views of a hedge-framed English garden with a fountain. The views from the house, perched at the top of Beachwood Canyon, are stunning.

Previous spread: The original ceiling of the formal living room has beams with stenciled paintings and figurative corbels. The window looks out over the canyon. A select few of Moby's expansive collection of globes are showcased on the bookshelves. The house is furnished with a host of Danish and French modern furniture.

Top left: Moby, photographed at the dining room table under a modern swing arm sconce, just one of the modern pieces that has given the house its personal style. *Top right:* A 1940s side chair sits beneath a framed blueprint of the original house plan. *Opposite:* The dining room has a simple Danish-modern dining table and chairs. The original coffered ceiling was restored during the renovation. The peaked soffit and window are a prominent architectural detail in the room.

Left: A Danish-modern sideboard is flanked by a pair of nickel lamps in the dining room. *Right:* A photograph of the house in the 1920s sits on a credenza in the guesthouse.

Previous spread: The John Lautner guesthouse, added to the property in 1961, serves as Moby's work space. The main floor is set up as a living space with a functioning kitchen.
Right: The fireplace is a signature example of Lautner's stonework.

VINCENT VAN DUYSEN

Belgian architect Vincent Van Duysen is known for creating buildings and residences worldwide with a remarkable sense of purity and a refined palette of materials. He creates spaces that exist at the intersection of art, architecture, and nature—structures that resonate profoundly in the modern world.

Educated at the Higher Institute of Architecture Sint-Lucas, Ghent, his architectural practice is currently based in Antwerp, Belgium. His areas of considerable expertise include domestic architecture, and the design of office and commercial spaces, as well as furniture and decorative objects for such leading international manufacturers as B&B Italia, Geiger, and Swarovski.

Van Duysen's own home is pure in the truest sense of the word—it is precisely designed, simple, and bold, reverberating with thoughtful tranquility. Each and every object has a a purpose, a reason behind its inclusion. Yet there is also a sense of comfort that radiates from every piece, especially those that are vintage or handmade, blending seamlessly with the modernist quality of the architecture. The harmony of colors and textures provides a sense of balance rarely seen in domestic spaces.

Dior creative director, Raf Simons, said the following of Van Duysen's home in *Interview* magazine: "Then there is your house in Antwerp, which I find purist but I don't find minimal—because there is nothing that disconnects the person from the environment. It's not a person versus the space—it's all one."

Indeed, his home is an extension of his own brilliant, multifaceted self, a physical manifestation of his progressive design philosophy. "I was much more attracted by interiors—the art of living—about colors, fabrics, materials, and about designing objects that belong inside the houses of people," Van Duysen says in the *Interview* piece. "Because for me, architecture was not this building or this construction, it was much broader. I like how it was decades ago when every single piece that you designed—a carpet, a lamp, a chair—all belonged to this one thing, a house."

While far from a luddite, Van Duysen tempers his use of technology. His inclination is to surround himself with natural materials, ones that connect the person to the object and to the home. "I like to surround myself with books," he says. "Not only in my library, but in the bedroom, living room, and kitchen. In most spaces in my home you will find books. This allows me to pick up a book at any moment, at any place. Through reading books, I am able to enter another's world while being inspired in a poetic way."

His work has been praised for its sincerity, its unfettered transparency, its ability to enliven environments with the unmistakable aura of integrity. And yet, Van Duysen is not an untouchable aesthete. He reveals that after a long day of work, his favorite activity is to sit with his beloved dachshunds Gaston and Loulou, open up a bottle of wine, and drink a glass by the fire. No matter how brilliantly high-minded the design may be, his home is, most fundamentally, a place to truly live.

Vincent Van Duysen designed this table for Home Saint Paul and paired it with rural Chinese stools. The artwork on the wall, by artist Tadashi Kawamata, incorporates complementary tones.

Left: The living room echoes the subtleties of the dining room, with touches of comfort from the linen upholstery. *Following spread, left:* Raw wood is used for coffee tables, and stacked books on multilevel side tables provide a perfect reading area.

Following spread, right, clockwise from top left: Van Duysen with his dog, Gasten; light reflected from the many windows onto the cream walls and floors leads one into the entrance and reception room; the walls of the TV/reading room are painted a shade of charcoal gray, complementing the velvet sofa which—along with the lower bench—is covered with an antique, hand-woven Turkish fabric; A white textured sculpture reinforces Van Duysen's use of objects, furniture, and art that all have a similar tactile quality.

MOURNING DOVES
Vincent Van Duysen

Right: Simple and clean lines are
reflected in the built-in bookcase
that surrounds the bed. The
tall shelving keeps the bedroom
feeling open and light, where
the side table—a raw wooden
block—introduces a juxtaposition of material and texture,
pairing beautifully with the
Iranian handwoven carpet.

The bowerbird is the master craftsman of the avian world. A prodigious
builder and collector, a male will
construct a complex haven of leaves,
moss, and twigs — a "bower" — and then
trick it out with feathers, shells, pebbles,
and berries to attract a mate. It's a love
nest in every sense of the word.

Boasting satiny plumage and cobalt
blue eyes, bowerbirds are known
to occupy a range of ecosystems, from
tropical rainforests to low-country
shrublands. But like these next three
subjects, wherever they roam, they
make their home.

Chapter 2

BOWERBIRDS

JOHN
DERIAN

John Derian lucked into one of those covetable New York City apartments that only a mixture of good timing and good karma opens doors to. The building, on Second Street in the East Village, is located advantageously near his two home décor stores, John Derian Company and John Derian Dry Goods. Over the years he got to know a long-standing tenant, an artist in her eighties named Louise. His good-hearted, inquisitive nature and their shared interests in art, collecting, and gardening formed a bond, and when she eventually moved out, he moved in.

He commenced a careful restoration, tearing out plywood to reveal original plank-wood subflooring, building out the bathroom and installing a vintage bathtub and sink, and painting walls a creamy alabaster. Eschewing the futuristic trappings of a generically sleek modern makeover, he lets the rough edges shine—a wall crack here, a bit of beautifully crumbling marble there—maintaining a look that feels true to the space's prewar heritage, and to his collector sensibility.

Derian started the John Derian Company in 1989, specializing in decoupage plates, platters, paperweights, coasters, and bowls (all handmade in his studio, where he employs a small staff of artisans). The business has grown to encompass vintage and antique pieces, both domestic and imported, bed and table linens, stationery, tableware, lighting, a diverse assortment of one-of-a-kind curios, as well as his own furniture line.

Derian is a born hunter and gatherer, a preserver of the peculiar and lovely ephemera that time leaves behind. World renowned for his decoupage plates depicting everything from Victorian writing desks to old valentines and animals, both real and fantastical,

he is drawn to evocative, soul-stirring images. In his stores and in his home, he curates the environment with a discerning yet welcoming eye.

"I like punctuations of color but stay clear of too much color," Derian says. Indeed, the space takes a dignified pass on "pops" of anything. Instead, its muted elegance is gracefully punctuated by gleaming brass fixtures, nautical imagery, or something as simple as a vintage easel smeared with oil paint.

In a serendipitous twist, the apartment faces the New York Marble Cemetery, the oldest public non-sectarian cemetery in New York City, named for its below-ground vaults made of solid white Tuckahoe marble. "I love the nook next to the window, where I can see out to the cemetery, which has no gravestones; it is just a beautiful wall surrounding a field."

He reveals that his favorite piece of art is a pencil drawing of a boy from the late 1700s. "It is so fresh and alive still," he says. "Also, I love the color and depth of landscape paintings."

When working, cooking, or entertaining, Derian's music preferences lean toward obscure 1970s New York disco and the soundtrack to the movie *Diva*. But his favorite leisure activity is to curl up in the nook and watch a movie. "I guess my section will be called a rook in the nook," he jokes. "Though I'm no crow."

John Derian's apartment in the East Village with original paint-spattered floors. A cabinet of found treasures sits next to a painted farm table. The window looks out onto the historic Marble Cemetery. *Following spread*: An antique tufted bench is the main seating area in Derian's living room. The original picture rails are employed with brass picture rods to hang a series of oil paintings.

Opposite: An antique demilune settee sits next to the fireplace in the bedroom. A piece of painted glass art hangs above the fireplace. This is a piece he purchased from the previous owner on a visit years ago. *Top left:* Derian, photographed in his bedroom. *Top right:* The vintage bathtub and sink were added to the apartment as well as period-appropriate bath fixtures.

Following spread, left: The work space of the house is filled with vintage images and ephemera. A beautifully weathered articulating lamp lights the space. *Following spread, right:* A vintage slop sink is used as the sink in the kitchen. The refrigerator is housed in a cabinet covered by a salvaged door.

Right: A simple framed line drawing hangs above the paneled wall of the dining area. *Opposite:* An antique iron bed and crystal chandelier adorn the bedroom. *Following spread, left:* The focal point of the foyer is a painted backdrop of curiosity drawers. An antique settee chandelier of found vintage parts and mirrors creates a romantic setting. *Following spread, right:* A collection of works by friend Hugo Guinness hangs above a fireplace in Derian's bedroom.

ANDREA BRUGI &
SAMINA LANGHOLZ

Many years ago, Denmark native Samina Langholz received an unexpected message from a Copenhagen clairvoyant. "The wise man predicted that one day I would settle in another country," she says. "I dismissed that flatly. I do not believe in that sort of prophecy."

But in 2004, on a beautiful summer evening on a visit to Montemerano, a small village in rural Tuscany, her skepticism was called into question. "I caught a glimpse of Andrea [Brugi] on the square in Montemerano, and instantly knew that my fate had caught up with me," she says. She didn't know a word of Italian, but decided to follow her heart, give notice at her job, and sell her car. Nine months later she was living out that doubtful prophecy, happily settled in another country and madly in love with Brugi.

Langholz fell not just for the man, but for his craft. An artisan of staggering talents, Brugi creates furniture, serving bowls, cutting boards, and exquisite curiosities crafted from found objects and raw materials that he finds in and around his home in Tuscany. He works at his family farmhouse, which dates back to 1678, in a back shed he's named the "laboratorio."

There he soaks wood for cutting boards in olive oils to make them stain-resistant while preserving their patina, and hand-carves chunky olive branches into salt dishes that resemble miniature tree trunks. Solid elm trunks are transformed into coffee tables. Simple garment racks are made from chestnut branches, also used by locals as horse paddocks. Vintage tools are taken apart and used as details, their rich metal accents elevating his pieces even further.

In Brugi's words, his work is "always created by a feeling. I never decide how a piece should look. It is the grain and shape of the piece of wood that determines the final result." In this way, Brugi conjures objects of pure function that also convey the idyllic rhythms of his world: ancient rooftops, ochre hills, gentle oaks, narrow village streets.

With so much beauty just outside the window, their home has been furnished in a relatively minimalist way, enlivened by their original creations, as well as carefully chosen antiques, flea market finds, and Scandinavian design classics. Most nights, jazz music floats from the speakers as Langholz pours coffee in her favorite Royal Danish porcelain, in that far-off country they both call home.

The living room of Brugi and Langholz's town house is simply furnished with a chesterfield sofa and Danish side table, letting the three-hundred-plus-year-old stone and beams be the focal point of this inviting space. *Following spread:* The kitchen/dining room features one of Brugi's reclaimed lumber dining tables.

Opposite: A Royal Copenhagen
porcelain bowl sits atop a
bookcase in the dining area.
A niche that was originally a
window houses a collection of
curious, artfully curated objects.
Right: The curving staircase
leading to the top floor of the
house, surrounded by original
stone walls.

Previous spread, left: The master bedroom consumes half of the top floor of the town house. The window overlooks the Tuscan valley below. Their daughter's dress hangs on a hanger, hand carved by Brugi. *Previous spread, right:* The master bed, unadorned, is complemented by a crystal chandelier and hanging bassinette.

Opposite: The work space on the top floor is host to a collection of objects, family photos, and nostalgic images. *Top left:* A pair of Danish flags mark the turf of transplanted Dane Langholz. An antique crystal chandelier is swagged above. *Top right:* The stone of the original house creates the shower walls. Brugi hand carved a wooden rod to serve as the shower curtain.

Opposite: A Poul Kjaerholm
chair sits next to the work table
that is home to a Santa Maria
statue. *Right:* Langholz and
Brugi, photographed with their
daughter, Gloria, in front of
their home.

CHRISTIANE PERROCHON & KASPAR VON ARX

The life of a ceramist in Tuscany may sound like a fantasy—or a luminously shot Diane Lane movie—but to artist and maker Christiane Perrochon it's a singular calling. She lives in Castiglion Alberti, an ancient villa in the Tuscan hills, where she creates revered stoneware and porcelain ceramics, thrown at the wheel, shaped by hand, and brought to vivid life with textural glazes.

Castiglion Alberti is located deep in Chianti country, proximate to Florence, Arezzo, and Siena, but far enough away from these cities to foster a sense of peaceful isolation. It was once a working church with an adjoining chapel and farmhouse. Today the ground floor houses Perrochon's ceramic atelier, with a showroom in the former chapel. The upper floors are the residence of the artist and her family.

She has a gift for conjuring colors that radiate an inner power and vibrancy, palettes rarely seen in stoneware. Her surroundings feed into her work, with the Tuscan light informing everything. "Here the light has a different quality," she says. "This hill is an extraordinary place. The colors are subtle and delicate. I find continuous nourishment in their hues."

Perrochon's passion for color first manifested during her studies at the École des Arts Décoratifs in Geneva. When she finished school she honed her craft and developed her own techniques. She began experimenting with firing her kiln at a higher temperature. At this time, natural colors were *de rigueur* in the ceramicist community and her work caused a sensation. "I made my strong blue, my strong pink, strong yellow, strong green; I was doing something against what I was taught," she says.

Five years after school, Perrochon and her husband Kaspar, also an artist, had the opportunity to move to Tuscany. Some locals questioned their desire to live and work high on a remote hill with no electricity, no running water, not even a serviceable road. But they felt right at home. The couple didn't have a lot of money, so they did what one does in the country: they got some sheep. She began shearing them and dyeing the wool, knitting extraordinary pieces.

From here she found that color was her ultimate inspiration; coaxing its transformative powers out of any material was to be her life's work. This philosophy can be seen in every aspect of her home and studio. Perrochon painted all the rooms with hand-mixed paints, including a fresco of pigment-derived pink in one hallway and a sunny living room wall created with ochre and sienna. She casted and glazed all the interior tiles and porcelain sinks. She refurbished the old chapel, fittingly, as there is no doubt something of the divine about the objects she creates.

It's a serene yet robust place, where dogs and cats drift in and out, and guests visit often for long, way-past-sunset dinners. In the spring, the aroma of fig trees fills the house; in the winter there's a constant smell of wood smoke and home-cooked meals. Antique rocking chairs, farmhouse tables, and oak armoires cohabitate tranquilly with Japanese light fixtures and Scandinavian chairs.

All told, Castiglion Alberti is infused with the same sense of inspired abandon that defines her work. "In this creative process one is constantly courting disaster," Perrochon says. "These are very particular glazes, very risky. At times, one gets closer to a desired color thanks to a simple flash of intuition."

The kitchen of ceramicist Christiane Perrochon and her husband, Kaspar von Arx. The floors are composed of handmade tiles that Perrochon created and painted specifically for the space. Modern chairs and ceiling fixture juxtapose with the centuries-old beams and walls.

Opposite: The breakfast room
with Mies van der Rohe chairs
is drenched in morning light.
The floors are a continuation of
the handmade painted tiles by
Perrochon. *Top left:* Perrochon
and Kaspar, photographed in the
studio's finish area, originally the
chapel of the villa. *Top right:* The
villa as seen from the back of
the property. The couple moved
to Tuscany from Switzerland in
the 1970s to pursue a more rural
life of farming and establishing
a studio.

Following spread, left: A
nineteenth-century sleigh bed
in the master bedroom.
Following spread, right: A Thonet
Bentwood rocker and Noguchi
lantern express the couples love
of mixing modern, sculptural
pieces with classic antiques.

Previous spread, right: The study where Perrochon works on sketches of new pieces and color palettes. *Previous spread, left:* The library houses a vast collection of pottery and craft books. In the doorway to a guest room, Moroccan fabric is draped for privacy.

Top: The morning view of the Tuscan valley from the terrace off of the kitchen. A local magpie that was saved as a chick by Kaspar visits them daily on the terrace. *Opposite:* Porcelain pieces are displayed in the dining room. Perrochon's grandmother was a porcelain painter in Switzerland. Their granddaughter displays a penchant for following in Perrochon's footsteps. *Following spread:* The holding area in the studio for finished pieces.

DITTE ISAGER & CHRISTIAN VANG

Danish photographer Ditte Isager's country house in Denmark is a small miracle, an eloquent take on the old saying "less is more."

"We bought the house thirteen years ago, and it looked very different from what it is now," Isager explains. "It was a very old little cottage, very romantic."

However it did lack a few things—namely running water and plumbing. Three years ago, Isager and her husband, Christian Vang, executed a substantial remodel. They did initial sketches and interior design schematics themselves. One ingenious solution was to create a studio space with a large glass door to infuse the house with natural light and air.

"We came up with the idea of putting a glass garage door in one wall," Isager explains. "In the summer, it's open all the time, and it makes the house feel double the size."

Other space limitations that might daunt some homeowners are seen as positives through the calm and cheerful worldview of Isager and Vang. "The kitchen is small but you can talk to your guests while you are cooking and see the sky," she says. The same sanguine attitude goes for the bedroom/bathroom. "I have always wanted a bathtub in my bedroom, and now I have it! We found an old lion-claw-foot tub and spent days removing layers and layers of old paint," she says.

Additionally, the couple built an outdoor shower, which they use until the frost comes. "It is the best, such a great way of starting the day," Isager says.

Throughout the cottage, the eye is drawn to a mix of clean, practical Nordic design, combined with flea market finds and organic colors and textures. "It is all very neutral and light. We wanted this to be a place of peace where we can relax," she says.

Outside, the beautifully rambling garden is another place of solace. "The garden is small, but we have all we need: apple, cherry, and hazelnut trees, a little herb garden in the back, and the most beautiful roses. I like the garden a bit messy," she says.

Since having their son, Wilder, the couple has been spending even more time in this idyllic place. "In Denmark babies sleep outside in the stroller in the daytime, and here he can sleep in the garden instead of walking him around in the stroller for hours," she says.

The couple also enjoys bonfires in the garden with friends and family. During the winter, the interior wood stove is constantly burning. When asked about her favorite moments in their home, Isager conjures a scene that is all the more beautiful for its simplicity: "A winter night, with the garden full of snow, lit up by the stars, music on the old B&O record player, and a pot of goulash on the wooden stove—that is magic."

A view from the dining area of Isager and Vang's cottage on the outskirts of Copenhagen. The campaign bed serves as a seating and napping spot in the afternoon sun.

Previous spread: The dining
area and kitchen are the hub of
the house. The kitchen cabinets
serve as axis, with bedroom
and bathroom on the other side.
The table and bench are by
Andrea Brugi, a dear friend of
the couple.

Top left: The dining area from
the main entrance to the
cottage. The rustic and modern
simplicity of the furniture
allows for cozy yet spare living
quarters. *Top right:* The
bathroom sink with collected
tiles as backsplash. *Opposite:*
The claw-foot bathtub is
essentially at the foot of the bed.
The water closet is the only
space in the cottage with a door.

Previous spread, left: A view to the bedroom from the front entrance. A small work area is nestled between the living and sleeping areas. *Previous spread, right:* A photograph by Isager hangs above the bed.

Top left: The outdoor shower with a plastic tarp serving as the shower curtain. *Top right:* A self-portrait of Isager and Vang in the outdoor dining area of their home. *Opposite:* A view of the cottage from the front garden.

LEIF
SIGERSEN

Copenhagen-born Leif Sigersen's specialties span industries and defy easy categorization. Set design, fashion editorial, advertising, interior design, high-end floral arrangements—he's a veritable creative chameleon. No matter what the medium, Sigersen's work has a beautifully baroque, surrealist tone that is also extremely tactile—you want to touch everything in the environments he creates.

One could say this sense of magical authenticity stems from his twin passions for floral design and antique objects. "Since I was a child, I bought flowers and plants at the flower market to decorate my room," Sigersen says. "When I was about twelve years old I was going to the flea market. So my home has always been filled with old stuff."

He studied under revered Danish florist Tage Andersen, and soon became a notable floral artist in his own right. To broaden his skill set, he worked as a stylist's assistant before opening the lauded boutique Gaven til Paven in a historic pavilion in King's Garden, Copenhagen.

In the early 2000s, Sigersen moved to New York and began work as an interior designer for shops, restaurants, and private homes, as well as a set designer for magazines and advertising. In 2006, he partnered with good friend/supermodel Helena Christensen to open Butik, a graceful West Village shop specializing in cutting-edge Danish clothing lines, rarefied flower arrangements, jewelry, and antiques in a bucolic, secret-garden setting.

"Once Stevie Wonder contacted Butik," Sigersen recalls. "He wanted me to create one of my special bouquets, which he had heard of. He added that it should 'smell wonderful.' I found that very sweet."

In 2010, Sigersen moved back to his native Copenhagen to focus on interior design. For the past several years, Sigersen's home has transformed into a hybrid workshop/studio. It's one continuous collection, a thriving work in progress, a never-ending labor of love.

"My own home probably never will be finished," he says. "But it is what keeps me going and inspires me. My home is my base, my nest."

The design of his home accentuates the inherent power of individual objects, whether crafted by hand or produced by industrial means. His style is wonderfully rambling, curated without an emphasis on prestige pieces. "It's not important that it's a fine old antique, it doesn't matter whether it's two or two hundred years old, it's more that it feels right to me, that it has the correct color, texture, and mood, and tells a story."

It's that innate sense of storytelling that makes his home such a surprising and alive-seeming place, full of unexpected visual jolts: a bushel of dried flowers, pieces of Americana, vintage children's clothes, machinery parts, a curiously lovely pile of old shoes. Indeed, it is as if every piece in his home is part of a grand spell that Sigersen happily conjures every day.

"I love funny old things, and sometimes, they are for me almost art pieces. Sometimes almost 'ugly' things can be much more interesting," he says.

A niche in the apartment where stacks of books and figures of inspiration have become a work space for Sigersen. The glass partition doubles as a banister to the spiral staircase. *Following spread:* The living space of the apartment is spare but adorned with beautiful antiques found at flea markets.

Right: Leif Sigersen photographed in his sitting room.

Left: The dining room of the top-floor flat. An antique "pie safe" houses objects as well as serving pieces. The white floors and clean lines of the dining room help keep the perfect balance of antique and modern.

Following spread, left: A tiny terrace allows room for the Sigersens to expand their collection of plants. *Following spread, right:* The kitchen with an antique wallpapering table used as an island. The modernity of the kitchen is a perfect juxtaposition, preventing the found objects from becoming clutter.

A beguiling bird, found a bit off the
grid and resplendent in electric blue and
poppy orange, the kingfisher displays
an air of stylish abandon as it struts up
and down riverbeds and shorelines.
Its most distinguishing characteristics are
a long, daggerlike bill and alert, bark
brown eyes.

A melodic, endearingly off-kilter
warble telegraphs its social nature as
well as its eccentricity — kingfisher
is the elusive, fascinating guest nobody
wants to leave the party.

Chapter 3

KINGFISHERS

CURTIS
KULIG

Artist Curtis Kulig's loft is bright and simple, awash in natural light. A far cry from hedonistic party lofts of decades past, it gives Kulig a sense of order and reprieve from the whirling momentum of his in-demand life. It's a place to rest from his travels, catch up on sleep, curl up in bed and draw, and, of course, create and collect art.

Born in North Dakota, Kulig was influenced early on by his uncle Philip Salvato, an American painter, and his father, Walter Kulig, a silk screener. Curtis began screen printing in his father's shop at the young age of twelve and moved to Los Angeles to pursue his art at nineteen. Today he lives and works in New York City where his signature "Love Me" campaign can be seen throughout the city's ever-evolving sprawl.

Inverting Milton Glaser's famous "I Heart NY" logo to reveal the essence of human desire, "Love Me" is fast becoming a twenty-first-century New York icon. It has made Kulig a rising star in both the art and commercial worlds, allowing him to shift between mediums while maintaining the message.

How, exactly, did inspiration strike? Kulig, who long has harbored a fascination with handwriting, started scripting "love me" in his journal, over and over again. He found something hypnotic and human about the two words, and the sweeping motion of the "M" that resembles a heart.

Next, he started painting it, first around Los Angeles and then in New York, where he relocated in 2008. "Love Me" can be seen in high-visibility intersections, such as the bombastic convergence of Broadway and Canal Street. It is a persuasive reminder of the primal need for empathy and intimacy, looming above a sea of iPhone-addled tweens and fake Louis Vuitton–seeking tourists like a soulful reproach.

"Love Me" can also be spotted on the streets of Berlin, Paris, and Tokyo, on large canvases in London, ablaze in bright neons in Hong Kong, and in collaborations with brands such as Nike, Obey Clothing, Smashbox cosmetics, Vans, and Urban Outfitters, among others.

Beyond these "collabs," he is also known for photography: intimate black-and-white Polaroid and 35-mm portraiture. Many of these portraits adorn the space, giving it a sense of liveliness and closeness. And "Love Me" in its many iterations (large canvases in rich acrylics, bronze and resin casted sculptures, electric red and white neons, and embroidered sneakers) is everywhere. His design style is pleasingly chaotic, rife with vintage finds and contemporary pieces, motorbikes and record players, decorative end tables, and old traveling trunks.

A kind soul who is considerably wiser than his skater-kid appearance might suggest, he radiates openness. It may sound like a cliché, but Kulig is a genuine "sensitive artist," as attested to by his multitude of friends, fans, and admirers, and by the respect and kindness with which he treats his subjects.

Of his unexpected success, Kulig told *Citizens of Humanity* magazine, "Right now, it's just my life. And it's growing faster and bigger than I could have ever imagined and so I just try to do the right thing every day and hope that it all keeps working out in my favor. I just try to paint every day. That's how it started and that's all I really need to continue."

Whether it's pieces he's made or pieces he collects, it is clear that art is not a vocation to him. It's sacred.

"Love Me" is artist Curtis Kulig's creative core. The phrase and font have become known worldwide. Pictured is a neon sign of the now-iconic image, and above are enlarged Polaroids by Maripol.

Opposite: Shelves in Kulig's loft house his art supplies and collected pieces. The vintage Puch moped is a recent acquisition. *Top:* Kulig, photographed in his downtown loft. *Following spread:* The dining table also serves as work space. It's host to vibrant dinners and inspired creations. A larger scale "Love Me" neon rests on the floor. A collection of vintage cameras (Kulig is also a photographer) are one of many assemblages on the shelves.

Last section spread: Kulig's studio, a few blocks east of his home, is a throwback to old New York artists' spaces. You can see between some of the floorboards to the space below. Several works in progress are idling around the studio.

DOUGLAS BENSADOUN

Douglas Bensadoun's French grandmother had a saying that has stuck with him: "*Comme tu fais ton lit tu dors.*" This translates roughly to: "You'll sleep as well as you've made your bed."

It's safe to assume Bensadoun sleeps just fine. The slyly charming, charismatic creative director of ALDO carries the torch from his father, Aldo Bensadoun, founder of the successful shoe company in Montreal in 1972. Now at the helm, Douglas is successfully leading the brand into the twenty-first century with a modern, energetic look and feel that's high-fashion and yet accessible.

He resides, fittingly, in a converted shoe factory in Montreal, a sprawling loft built in 1948. The open space features intentionally strong colors and design choices. A particularly striking element is a series of stained-glass window shades—warmly hued panels that cast tones of amber, crimson, and gold throughout the house, depending on weather and time of day.

Bensadoun believes that light and color in his home acutely affect his mood: "If it's positive, I let it in and take run of the place."

This interchangeable lighting provides amazing prisms and glows, but there's also a lingering darkness in the décor—a deep contrast. In his bedroom, coal gray walls and a mass of hanging lamps create his very own constellations. It's a deliberate choice that appears effortless and organic. Altogether it conjures a simula-crum of his personality: a little outward cockiness with a sweet, thoughtful side.

His home offers both inspiration and respite from everyday life. Some of his best ideas have come while taking a nap on the daybed with the breeze coming in from the sliding doors, his handsome little dog Walter at his side. He's also host to impromptu dinners and ad hoc gatherings, where he dubs the massive kitchen counter "command central."

As far as furnishings, Bensadoun's most prized possession is a pair of original Hans J. Wegner Papa Bear chairs. "It took me forever to find them. I found them at the same time in the strangest of places, in even stranger circumstances," he says. Less mysteriously obtained pieces include salvaged factory stools, a lovely orange mid-century loveseat, and a portrait of a fox as wily executive.

And he loves sunflowers. "They follow the light and they look beautiful in a very simple way."

When asked for his favorite saying or philosophy, his response is typically atypical, quoting not Rumi or Nietzsche, but instead a lyric from Canadian band The Tragically Hip: *Violins and tambourines / This is what we think they mean / It's hard to say, it's sad but true / I'm kinda dumb and so are you.*

It's the self-effacing playfulness that makes his home so enigmatic. For such an ascendant talent, he remains remarkably grounded. His ideal night? "Drinking some nice wine, and making a big salad with lots of friends with all the doors and windows open."

Retractable glass doors allow the sun and breeze to infuse the main floor of the converted loft. An open living room is situated between the dining area, kitchen, and entryway, allowing for a continuous flow.

Opposite: The dining area is a favorite gathering place for impromptu get-togethers and dinners. Yellow casts from the windows create a gradual shift in light throughout the day and evening.

Top left: The installation on the wall is by Cuban artist Damian Aquiles. According to Bensadoun, Aquiles came over to the house and requested a bottle of tequila and some 140 BPM techno. Bensadoun says, "I obliged and joined him, and he went to work [installing the piece];" *Top right:* A free-floating black-painted wall functions as a bike rack, and creates a sense of separation between the entryway and the kitchen.

Top left: Bensadoun in his home, replicating the painting by Richard Ahnert that hangs above his desk. "It was his second show; he had six or seven pieces on display, all he'd ever done at that point. I fell in love with the fox having writer's block—reminded me of, well, me."

ALLISON SHEARMUR

Allison Shearmur may be best known as a bona fide Hollywood power player—she's a successful film producer and production and development executive with such massive successes as *The Hunger Games* and the *Bourne* trilogy under her belt—but she's also a prolific art collector and a modern-day aesthete with a sharp eye for fashion and interior design. It all connects, somehow: her refined taste flows into her various passions, with results that, like her blockbuster films, are smart, thought-provoking, sophisticated, and inclusive.

Her art collection is formidable—the Shearmurs have loaned pieces to the Tate Modern and MoMA—but the interior design of her Los Angeles home, where she lives with her husband and children, is not. "Our home is mostly white with splashes of bright color that come from the art hung all over the house," she says. "I like the feeling of peace that comes from living in a white space filled with sunlight."

And it's not exclusively gallery works that grace the walls (although, give them time): "I also love bursts of colors from the children's artwork in the kitchen and the swaths of blue, yellow, orange, and red from the paintings," she explains. "Whether it is a quiet water-color that my daughter has painted or a wild net of red and green paint on a Kusama, I feel stimulated by the energies of all the art."

Shearmur's favorite place in the house is undoubt-edly the kitchen, where an old oak table is surrounded by vintage Adnet chairs, their ripped leather is seen as happy battle scars from her children's boisterous wear and tear. She chose dark burgundy marble countertops and a vintage green stove to evoke the colors of the iconic Musso & Frank Grill on Hollywood Boulevard, where she had her first meal when she moved to LA.

"I also love our balcony that looks out on downtown Los Angeles, its hazy Raymond Chandler-esque view," she says. "Again, very Los Angeles."

It's a home that also has the most priceless element of all: comfort. "Kids must be able to run around with their friends, parents need to find quiet places to read and talk, and friends should feel welcomed when they sit at your table for a meal. I also feel sunlight can make any room inviting and lift you up."

They love to entertain and regularly throw big parties where guests flow in and out onto the balcony: "Our favorite gatherings involve musicians playing their music live in the house," she says. "My husband's piano is a centerpiece in our home."

When asked about her motto when it comes to the house, Shearmur quotes Charles Dickens, no slouch in understanding the vital role of domestic happiness: "Home is a name, a word, it is a strong one; stronger than magician ever spoke, or spirit ever answered to, in the strongest conjuration."

The living room of Allison Shearmur's home is stately and minimal. The bookshelves contain an amazing array of art books as well as smaller collected pieces. The shelves were constructed to fit the Laura Owens piece, featured in the image.

Top left. Shearmur, photographed in the sitting area of her closet, surrounded by a few of her favorite pieces from her extensive wardrobe collection. *Top right:* A dress hangs in Shearmur's custom closet, with linen-upholstered doors and nail-head-pattern detail. *Opposite:* A Nan Goldin photograph hangs in the dining room of Shearmur's Los Angeles home.

Following spread: The master stairwell foyer is home to some treasured pieces including (*left*), a Kurt Kauper painting holds court at the end of the hall, and (*right*), an Edgar Bryan which is hung above the passage to the main foyer.

An Elliot Hundley hangs above
the grand piano in the living
room. The doors to the left lead
to the breakfast terrace with a
view of downtown Los Angeles.
Following spread, left: Shearmur's
office on the main floor of the
house. *Following spread, right:*
The rotunda is used as another
sitting room in the house.
The lamp on the side table is
a Fortuny. The French doors
lead out to the main terrace
with sweeping views of
greater Los Angeles, which
the Shearmur's describe as
"Raymond Chandler-esque."

151

Left: In the powder room
hangs a photo by Cindy
Sherman from early work
she did as an art student.
Opposite: The master vanity
with hand-painted wallpaper.

The seashore-dwelling sandpiper has dapper brown-and-white-spotted plumage, a swift gait, and a deep kinship with all things aquatic. Distinctive for its gender-swapping parenting style, in which females forage and males raise the young, this lithe, industrious shorebird is a welcome sight on land and sea, and in all the mysterious spaces in between.

These homes represent the ancestral pull to reside near bodies of water, and their inhabitants are just as creative, convention-breaking, and enigmatic as the agile sandpiper.

Chapter 4

SANDPIPERS

ROGAN
GREGORY

"I am a maker."

The humble strength of this statement is evident in every square foot of Rogan Gregory's Montauk home. A lauded fashion designer, sustainability advocate, visual artist, and furniture maker, he crafted virtually everything in the house by hand: wooden bowls in the pantry, artwork on the walls, and benches, tables, and chairs. He learned the fundamentals of woodworking from his father, and has become a prodigious craftsman.

His dwelling is somewhat intimidating from the outside, a flat-black cinderblock monolith. However, he lets bamboo and winding wisteria run rampant, providing an earthy, sensual contrast. Gregory expects one day the native fauna will simply take over ("They are conquering all man-made things," he says). Inside, the palette softens to sandy blonds, natural woods, and talc-white walls.

A stack of surfboards leans casually against the doorway near a low bench where visitors can slip out of their shoes—who wouldn't want to feel their feet treading on the gorgeously bare wood floors? Throughout the artfully spare interior, one becomes aware of unforced juxtapositions: black and white sculptures, scattered antlers and succulent plants, petrified wood and serving bowls. His aesthetic and life, including his eponymous clothing line and stores, is all steeped in the same graphic simplicity. In the

words of his web site, "ROGAN combines soulful minimalism with traditional quality."

Gregory's devotion to objects of purpose and substance pervades the house. He has cultivated a space where the sculptural meets the functional, best encapsulated by his favorite furniture piece, a stable table and bench fashioned from reclaimed old-growth pine trees of the mid-south. "It's one of the first pieces of furniture I made and I'm sure I will be handing it down to my daughter," he says. An outdoor shower and custom studio/woodworking shop are other highlights of this halcyon abode.

Inside and out, he cares meticulously for orchids and other flowering plants. "Life-loving lilies never disappoint," he says. The scent of cedar floats through the space, its moody tones—especially when mixed with the utilitarian scent of gear oil in his workshop—recall the forest landscapes of his youth in Colorado and Canada. Above all, his home is one of contemplation and dedication to art, design, craft, and the enduring power of using your hands.

The living room area of the open floor plan in the top level of Gregory's Montauk home. A collection of antlers lays beneath a bench that was built by Gregory with a gathering of turned wooden bowls that he also made in his woodworking shop.

Top left: A detail of Gregory's turned wooden bowls. *Top right:* Plaster reliefs of seashell forms, also created by the artist, hang on the wall in the main living space. *Opposite:* Gregory's daughter, Gray, has lunch at the sturdy wood table, one of her father's first pieces, which will someday be passed down to her. The wooden sculpture on the table is another creation by Gregory.

Following spread: The daybed in the main living space is the perfect spot for lazy afternoons. It's surrounded by numerous sculptures and works in progress by Gregory. The wooden mobiles hanging in the space are recent works.

Top: Gregory, photographed in his workshop. His love of woodworking is credited to his father, who taught him the fundamentals that have allowed him to become a master craftsman.

Opposite: His outdoor table and benches sit under an unruly wisteria. The terrace is off of the main living space and serves as a dining area during summer months. The overgrown plant life is a key ingredient to the overall aesthetic of the property.

DOUG LLOYD

The most common question Doug Lloyd gets asked about his Amagansett home is, "How can you leave?" Parting from this idyllic beach retreat must be sweet sorrow indeed. Floor-to-ceiling sliding doors open from the kitchen onto a terrace, swimming pool, and views of Gardiners Bay, providing an elegant transparency that infuses rooms with the colors of the sea, sand, woods, and clouds.

And yet, duty calls. As founder and creative director of Lloyd & Co., a fashion and beauty branding and advertising agency with clients including Gucci, Oscar de la Renta, Bottega Veneta, and Adidas Y-3, he must divide his time between frenetic New York City and pastoral Amagansett. But when he's here, it's like another world.

"On one side, it is like a tree house nestled in a pine forest; the other, it's all open sky and water," Lloyd says of the sleek one-story house, designed by Frederick Stelle and Michael Lomont of Stelle Architects. Embracing nature is a thread throughout— from the African teak walls to the neutral textured rugs on the floor, and the location of the house itself, encased in the pines as though it were always a part of the ecosystem.

The furniture is an unpretentious mix of Danish and American mid-century, "But not the greatest hits," he clarifies. "It's all meant to be functional, easy, and low, so as not to obstruct the views." While the space evokes quietude, Lloyd's home is not a hushed retreat—on the contrary, he built it for entertaining. "It's a very easy house to have friends over to," he says. He has no shortage of appreciative guests in the summer months, and beyond.

The kitchen is a well-trafficked communal area connecting the living room, dining room, and patio. During the spring and summer, guests wander indoors and out in a continual flow, while in the winter months, a fire crackles as guests gaze out at the wintery night sky through the glass windows.

Along with fresh Montauk daisies, he enlivens the space with wild sea grass and sunflowers, bringing the natural world even further inside. Lloyd reveals his favorite scent is that of Oud wood burning, reminiscent of "the smell of being outdoors under a starry sky in either the southwest or Morocco."

Perhaps it is that rare fusion of escapism and hominess, the wild and the carefully contained that makes this house such a euphoric place to call home away from home.

Nestled between a glen of pines and open views of the bay, Doug Lloyd's home in Amagansett, New York, is an idyllic retreat. The doors open on both sides to allow the full feeling of being surrounded by nature. A large cast-iron bowl is a nest to a collection of magazines.

Opposite: The living room is artistically sparse. As it is part of the open floor plan, the lack of art allows the view of the bay to become the primary focal point. The coffee table has one of many collections of found foliage: sea shells, antlers, pebbles, and feathers, to name of a few of his calming still lifes. *Top left:* Lloyd photographed in the guest hallway. *Top right:* A shelf with a collection of treasured objects.

Following page, left: The dining room is earthy and elegant. An extension of the open living space, the doors open to the "forest side" of the property. *Following page, right:* The kitchen is a cook's dream. In one direction you are facing the pines and in the other, you are facing the bay. It's the perfect spot for guests to hang out while Lloyd is making dinner. The wood ceiling warms and balances the modern cabinets and appliances.

Top left: Shelves in the den with
a collection of pottery, favored
photos, and another gathering
of natural objects. *Top right:*
A detail moment against the
backdrop of wood paneling in
the den.

Opposite: The master bedroom detail. Its composition
is a masterpiece of tranquility
and simplicity.

MADS & CECILIE NØRGAARD

"I live on a houseboat with my wife and my two kids. I swim in the sea every morning."

It sounds like the beginning to a particularly sunny folk tale, but it is actually Danish fashion designer Mads Mathias Nørgaard's daily routine. He and his wife Cecilie, who is a gender and educational sociologist, and their family live on a houseboat on the Baltic Sea, just outside of Copenhagen proper. The Nørgaards have happily resided in a bright, casually elegant three-story nautical home for fifteen years.

It's a loving home, a safe harbor, a place that communicates a sense of pure joy and daily discovery. A white spiral staircase connects all three floors, and the décor has that eclectic-sophisticate quality that the Scandinavians pull off so deftly. It's also something of a floating art gallery, with paintings and sketches on almost every wall, and loads of rare books, sculptures, and the happy detritus of the creatively engaged.

One could say design is in Nørgaard's blood. His father, Jørgen Nørgaard, is a notable Danish designer—his flagship boutique, Nørgaard paa Strøget, is often considered "the APC of Denmark." Like father like son: along with being director and owner of the fashion house Mads Nørgaard, with men's and women's collections sold all over the world, Nørgaard has released a definitive Danish fashion encyclopedia and sits on the Danish Design Council and the board of the Vega Concert Hall in Copenhagen. A huge proponent of the Danish fashion scene, he is passionate about providing original pieces at accessible price points. "I have a responsibility to try to help people find what they want and like, not to tell them what to wear," he says.

Just as he creates fashion that's meant to be worn, not merely ogled on a runway, so is his home a place to be experienced—a place to truly live. Its warmth and inclusiveness conjure up a sense of clever domesticity, a freedom from convention that's not self-consciously "bohemian" at all. It's also the ideal venue for dinner parties, casual and formal alike. Many nights, music drifts out across the water as people mingle, have cocktails, and dine, fireplace ablaze.

In keeping with his egalitarian spirit, the children's rooms are no less astonishing and art-filled than any other room. There is a healthy sense of whimsy everywhere, with surprising bursts of color. The Nørgaard's artwork and furniture collection contains many serious design pieces, but the overall mood of the interior is fun and playful. One might find funny plastic figurines hanging on a chandelier—or a pack of cigarettes stuck on an Ólafur Elíasson light fixture.

The family's exuberance and generosity is palpable to all who step aboard—they've found their own version of the good life, and they're not leaving port anytime soon.

The dining area of the Nørgaard's houseboat in the Baltic Sea in Copenhagen. The doors lead to a deck/living area with a view of the harbor.

Previous spread: In the center of the houseboat is a spiral staircase that leads up to the master bedroom suite and down to the children's rooms and a common area. The gallery wall to the left is filled with collected pieces of art by friends and family. The door on the far left leads to the gangplank that connects them to land.

Opposite: The open kitchen has an island of storage shelves as the prep area. A papier-mâché horse head quietly oversees the cooking. *Top:* Mads and Cecilie Nørgaard photographed in their motorboat in the harbor.

Top left: A collection of art pieces is on the top of a bookshelf in the main living space. Wooden figures stand side by side in a porthole window. *Top right:* A collage of their children's art and postcards are neatly pinned amid found objects *Opposite:* The office space in the master suite has a view of neighboring boats and the harbor.

Following spread, left: A sitting area in front of the bookshelves also serves as the foyer table. The clamshell-like chandelier above the table is a resting place for easy-to-reach necessities. *Following spread, right:* The view of the walkway, gangplank, and houseboat as seen from the mainland.

The night owl is an otherworldly creature indeed. Known for nesting in barn lofts, attics, and church steeples, its shadow across the sky at night or just before dusk evokes a sense of ancient wisdom, a shortcut to the spirit world.

Here, explore two homes that conjure this twilight creature's beauty and mystery. Each piques curiosity, provokes strong emotions, and leaves a lovely, enigmatic feeling that lingers—like the flash of a half-remembered dream.

Chapter 5

NIGHT OWLS

BILL
MULLEN

Transcending the label "fashion stylist," Bill Mullen is a force of nature in the industry, putting his distinctive stamp on such publications as *Italian Vogue*, *Numéro*, *Vanity Fair*, and *T* magazine. Whether stripped-down minimalist, wildly tribal, or deeply sensual, his work is the essence of provocative—it makes you look twice. Mullen is also a design consultant, cat lover, and certified prince of darkness.

His Upper West Side apartment is best described as artfully macabre. There is no barrier between his refined-gothic personal style and interior design aesthetic—the two are symbiotic. The furniture is a rich mix of vintage and avant-garde modern, and the majority of artwork is by friends, or has been gifted to him by someone he loves.

His palette is comprised of three colors: black, white, and red. Black is, of course, the dominant anti-color. "I'm from a generation where wearing black meant something," Mullen says. "There's no beige or gray or middle ground. This is a palette that drives a hard bargain." He loves the contrast of pitch-dark pieces against white walls and the shifting shadows they create.

"My favorite house of all time is the Addams Family house in the old *New Yorker* cartoons," he says. "There is magic in the darkness." Indeed, the space has a kinetic energy. "It's a world of mystery and nighttime visitors, shadow lurkers, witches, vampires, and secret friends. It's romantic and extreme."

Mullen's favorite space is the living room. As he puts it, "It's the room of a chic vampire living in Manhattan." His black parrot, Morticia, lives there.

A charcoal drawing of a raven by his friend Eric Nash adorns one wall, and every surface holds a wicked surprise—there is no shortage of death's heads. The rug is a patchwork of red and black, and a blood-red cross holds court over the fireplace, flanked by more moody art and books upon books.

Mullen's most beloved piece? The Smoke Chair by Maarten Baas. "To me, it is everything I love rolled up in a chair. It's black and fucked up and new but old and wicked... it seems like something out of a horror movie. And because of the burned wood, it's unique."

Take a detour into a guest bedroom and find a pop art take on a Día de los Muertos shrine. Wander into the dining room and see an old library table anchoring the space, creating a gathering area and work station: "I work on it, draw on it, spread out stuff. There's always a cat on there shredding the *New York Times*."

A crimson leather chesterfield is on standby for languid guests. A snake lamp, a wild octopus floor lamp, a tiki lamp, and a set of skull lamps by Blackman Cruz give the space a dreamily demented glow. "I don't usually go for 'high design'—I like old things," Mullen says. "But the place is really filling up with some fantastic pieces. Some of it scares some people, but I don't care. At all."

The main living area is one of Mullen's favorite rooms. It's all about black in there, including his beloved black parrot Morticia. She is sensitive to strangers, so one must enter very slowly in order for her to become comfortable.

Top left: A photo of Bob Dylan sits next to a black and white skull. Mullen's mix of new and old is another signature of this unexpected apartment on the Upper West Side: a little rock and roll, fashion, with a wicked eye for strange and unusual beauty. *Top right:* Mullen with his black parrot Morticia, who stood very still for her portrait.

Opposite: A vintage leather chesterfield sits at one end of the dining room, alongside wooden shelves that house many of Mullen's books, taxidermy, photos of shoots he has styled, and his fantastical collections of vintage African pieces. This room serves as a dining room as well as a place to relax with books, newspapers, work, and cats.

ATHENA &
VICTOR
CALDERONE

Situated amid sea and sky, fields and farmhouses, Athena and Victor Calderone's Amagansett home was a labor of love from the start. This mid-century ranch house was in critical condition when they purchased it in 2009, but thankfully most of its elegant structure was sound. The Calderones channeled their own design ingenuity and enlisted the help of Bates + Masi Architects to create a graceful, glass-enclosed oasis for friends and jet-setting guests—as well as a peaceful nest for their family.

It's a place for early evening cocktails and lingering dinner parties. It's also a quiet retreat where their son Jivan can skateboard and surf. Amagansett's pastoral landscape infuses the house with stillness, a true sense of sanctuary. The choices in color and texture are informed by rocky coastlines, Scandinavian design, tactile and raw materials—as well as by the pair's artistic temperaments.

Victor is a music producer (he has produced and remixed tracks for Madonna, Beyoncé, and Sting, among others) and a renowned DJ, playing elite nightclubs and major international festivals. Athena is cofounder of interior design firm Rawlins Calderone Design, which curates high-end residential interiors as well as designing retail and hospitality projects in and around New York City. She prides herself on pairing the unexpected in life, design, and food, best exemplified by her thriving blog, Eye-Swoon.

"I am a visual creature, always on the lookout for inspiration," Athena says. "There are so many layers to creativity, in the food we create, how we dress, the rooms we live in."

Indeed, one theme that reverberates throughout the décor of the house is that of *layering*—in the living room you'll find Moroccan rugs, vintage American chairs, Belgian linen sofas, and a bench from an old railroad. The couple is devoted to creative reuse, sourcing reclaimed lumber for the walls, weaving rich old rope through a digitally fabricated framework in the ceiling, and utilizing an industrial pallet as a coffee table. There's a warm weight to every room, a safe, moored feeling.

"I am very much inspired by Scandinavian design," Athena says. "The neutral palettes and pure tones remind me of the sea and the sky and the earth. I like contrasting elements too: black chairs juxtaposed against pale, natural woods, or a shocking pop of color."

When it comes to art and home accessories, modern pieces sit agreeably next to vintage finds and natural curiosities. The Calderones like to travel, and are especially drawn to the islands off the coast of Greece, Italy, and Spain. They always bring something home—cockleshells, ceramics, local oddities—providing more unexpected touches.

The heart of the home is the unfussy kitchen, rife with reclaimed barn wood. "I am passionate about cooking local, seasonal food and gathering around the kitchen island," Athena says. "I love the Amagansett farm stands, the journey of starting with a simple combination of fresh ingredients and playing with flavors to create your own unique dish."

While their home is pretty close to "architecturally perfect" it is also infused with a vibrant sense of idiosyncrasy, the joy of the off-kilter. Perhaps this is best expressed by the Calderones' motto: "Live your life with grace, compassion, and honesty. Don't think too much. Find what it is about yourself that you love, and remember that in times of angst, laugh often, play often, lose yourself often."

The Calderones' dining room is situated proximate to the living room, with sliding glass doors that open out to the bucolic backyard.

VANITY FAIR PORTRAITS

Opposite: The master bath-room echoes elements from the rest of the house, with rope ceilings, reclaimed wood, and leather pulls for the cabinets— all evoking a sense of warmth and texture.

Top left: The rope detail covers the window, allowing for privacy as well as a beautiful cast of shadow. *Top right:* Athena, Victor, and their son Jivan, all of whom often hang outside. The house was built to encourage as much outdoor living as indoor.

First published in the United States of America
in 2014
by Rizzoli International Publications, Inc.
300 Park Avenue South
New York, NY 10010
www.rizzoliusa.com

Art © Ditte Isager
Text © Sarah Sophie Flicker, Mayer Rus,
Kim Ficaro, Todd Nickey, and Heather Wagner

Design: Rational Beauty,
Jeanette Abbink and Emily CM Anderson
Editor: Julie Schumacher
Writer: Heather Wagner
Production: Colin Hough-Trapp

Typeset in Lyon, designed by Kai Bernau
and Marian, designed by Paul Barnes
from Commerical Type Foundry.

ISBN: 978-0-8478-4243-8
Library of Congress Catalog Control Number:
2013947775

2014 2015 2016 2017 / 10 9 8 7 6 5 4 3 2 1

Printed in China

Acknowledgments

Kim Ficaro: I would like to thank Karyn Starr, Gary
Johnson, Winnie Beattie, Rob Magnotta, Chloe
Walsh, Joanna Troccoli, Ditte Isager, and Christian
Vang for their endless support, love, and family.
And to my parents, Roey and Tony Ficaro, and my
brother Jason, for their trust and always believing
in any and all of my dreams; I am beyond grateful
and inspired by you.

Todd Nickey: I would like to thank Greg Holcomb,
Amy Kehoe, and my parents, Lois and Smitty, for
all of their love and support.

Ditte Isager: I would like to thank Pippa and Jon for
being the most amazing tech and assistant that I
could wish for—you are my dream team! The Edge
crew, Rob you are the best—I'm a lucky girl!
Christian, thank you for your patience, for always
being there for me no matter where in the world.
Wilder, who was in my belly throughout this shoot,
and with his presence now, he makes me the
happiest mum in the world.

Kim, Todd, and Ditte would like to thank Sandra
Gilbert, Kayleigh Jankowski, Tricia Levi, Charles
Miers, Ellen Nidy, Anthony Petrillose, and Lynn
Scrabis at Rizzoli, and Kacy Strand and Erin Nicole
Graf at Edge Reps., and Christian Vang and all
at Werkstette.

A special acknowledgment to Samina Langholz
and Andrea Brugi, we feel honored to have stepped
into your beautiful studio in Italy and witness all
the beauty that was made there.